DANGEROUS DRUGS

COCAINE
AND CRACK

KATIE MARSICO

Cavendish
Square
New York

Published in 2014 by Cavendish Square Publishing, LLC
303 Park Avenue South, Suite 1247, New York, NY 10010

Library of Congress Cataloging-in-Publication Data
Marsico, Katie.
Cocaine and crack / by Katie Marsico.
p. cm. — (Dangerous drugs)
Includes index.
ISBN 978-1-62712-369-3 (hardcover) ISBN 978-1-62712-370-9 (paperback)
ISBN 978-1-62712-371-6 (ebook)
1. Cocaine abuse — Juvenile literature. 2. Crack (Drug) — Juvenile literature. 3. Drug abuse – Juvenile literature. I. Marsico, Katie, 1980-. II. Title.
HV5810 M34 2014
362.298—dc23

EDITORIAL DIRECTOR: Dean Miller
SENIOR EDITOR: Peter Mavrikis
SERIES DESIGNER: Kristen Branch

Photo research by Kristen Branch

The photographs in this book are used by permission and through the courtesy of: Cover photo by © Ted Foxx/Alamy; © Ted Foxx/Alamy, 1; Jeff Kravitz/FilmMagic/Getty Images, 4; Steve Wisbauer/Brand X Pictures/Getty Image, 7; © Jordi Camí/age fotostock, 9; © Linh Hassel/age fotostock, 11; John H. Stocksdale/William Stewart Halsted/ihm.nlm. nih.gov/images/B14034, 11; KiloByte/Cocaine for kids/en.wikipedia, 12; ROMEO GACAD/AFP/Getty Images, 13; Psychonaught/Crack Ingredients/Own work, 15; Frederick M. Brown/Getty Images Entertainment/Getty Images, 18; Otto Greule Jr/Hulton Archive/Getty Image, 17; © David Cole/Alamy, 19; Lisa Wahman/Panther Media/age fotostock, 20; Laurence Mouton/ès/SuperStock, 20; SuperStock/SuperStock, 20; National Institute on Drug Abuse/Soa 014 large/drugabuse.gove/publications/science-addiction/drugs-brain, 22; © Krzysztof Kruz/Alamy, 25; NBC via Getty Images/NBCUniversal/Getty Images, 26; Nathan Watkins/E+/Getty Images, 29; James Heilman, MD/Vasculitis/Own work/Creative Commons Attribution-Share Alike 3.0 Unported license/GNU Free Documentation License, 31; Christa Brunt/E+/Getty Images, 33; Comstock/Comstock Images/Getty Images, 34; AP Photo/Al Behrman, 37; © Jim West/age fotostock, 41; Robert Nickelsberg/Getty News Images/Getty Images, 43; © Richard Wright/Lithium/age fotostock, 47; Blend Images/Hill Street Studios/the Agency Collection/Getty Images, 48; © Lawrence Manning/Lithium/age fotostock, 49; Bruce Ayres/The Image Bank/Getty Images, 51; © Jeff Greenberg/Alamy, 55.

Printed in the United States of America

Contents

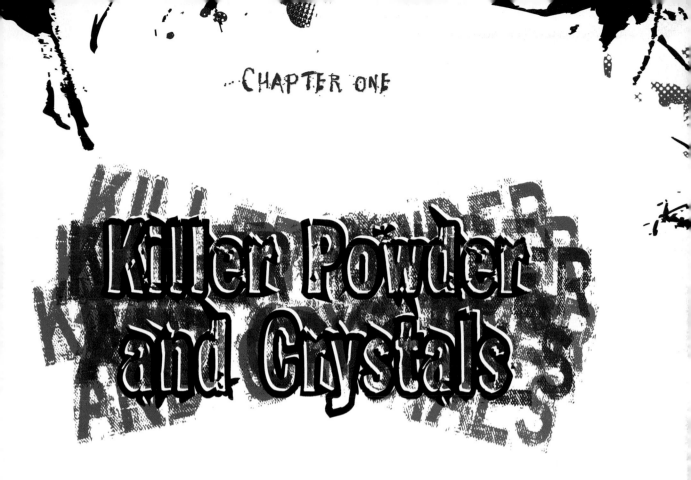

CHAPTER ONE

Killer Powder and Crystals

ON FEBRUARY 11, 2012, POP MUSIC FANS around the world grieved when news broke that award-winning singer Whitney Houston was dead at the age of forty-eight. Police and paramedics found the musician's lifeless body in a hotel room in Los Angeles, California. They also discovered a white powdery substance scattered around her bathroom, along with other evidence of possible drug use.

Left: Whitney Houston, one of the world's top-selling artists, fought a long, public battle with drugs and alcohol.

5

Months later, Chief Coroner Investigator Craig Harvey revealed that Houston had died as a result of heart disease, drowning—and a powerful **stimulant** called **cocaine**. Sadly, rumors of her drug abuse were nothing new. In 2006, Houston's sister-in-law Tina Brown shared several disturbing details of the star's **crack** habit with the media. Crack is cocaine that users smoke in the form of rocks or crystals.

"She won't stay off the drugs," Brown complained. "It's every single day. It's so ugly. Everyone is so scared she is going to [**overdose**]. . . . She spends her days locked in her bedroom amid piles of garbage, smoking crack . . . ." Much of the public found it hard to imagine that this description was accurate. How could the same smiling, elegant woman who had built a successful career as a recording artist, producer, actress, and model be **addicted** to crack?

Unfortunately Houston's death was a renewed wake-up call to the world about the dangers of cocaine. Not everyone who uses the stimulant is a wealthy, famous celebrity. Crack and any other form of cocaine have a devastating—and sometimes even deadly—impact on men, women, and children from every walk of life.

These individuals are often trapped in a cycle of addiction. They break the law to abuse cocaine because

6

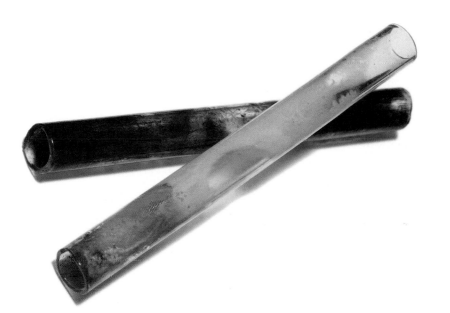

Crack is a low-cost, highly addictive drug that is usually smoked out of a pipe.

they become physically and mentally **dependent** on it. As a stimulant it creates a sense of increased alertness and energy. Cocaine also numbs physical pain and causes users to experience a feeling of intense happiness or excitement known as **euphoria**. Yet using the drug leads to a wide variety of health issues, as well, including emotional disturbances and problems that affect a person's heart, brain, and lungs.

Nevertheless, the National Survey on Drug Use and Health (NSDUH) reported that 637,000 Americans tried cocaine for the first time within twelve months of being interviewed in 2010. NSDUH researchers estimated that 83,000 of these users did crack. A separate study conducted by the Partnership for Drugfree.org revealed that, in 2012, approximately 7 percent of US teens admitted to having gotten high off of some form of cocaine during the previous year.

It's possible that not every one of these teenagers will go on to become a full-blown addict. Those that do will eventually need more and more cocaine to feel the same burst of energy and pleasure. Meanwhile, those teens that avoid addiction are still in danger of discovering how abusing the stimulant even once involves serious risks—and sometimes tragic consequences.

From Coca Plant to Popular Drug

Like many illegal drugs, cocaine did not start out with a reputation for being evil and addictive. This stimulant is made from the leaves of the South American coca plant. Experts believe that local people were already aware of its powers thousands of years ago and relied on the shrub to practice both medicine and religious rituals. Chewing the leaves fought hunger and boosted alertness and stamina,

8

The coca plant has played an important role in native South American culture for more than a thousand years.

or enduring strength and energy. It also soothed an upset stomach and numbed pain.

Throughout the eighteenth and nineteenth centuries, Europeans and Americans became more curious about the possible medical uses of the coca plant. In the mid-1800s, a scientist named Albert Niemann succeeded in extracting, or removing, a white powder from the leaves. He named it cocaine and, placing some of it upon his tongue, was impressed by its numbing effect. By the 1880s, scientists had started mixing Niemann's powder with a strong chemical called hydrochloric acid. The result was cocaine hydrochloride—

a salt that was far more powerful as a stimulant and pain-killer than chewed coca leaves.

During the last half of the nineteenth century, much of the medical community thought of cocaine as a wonder drug and a miracle of modern science. Surgeons used it as an **anesthetic**, and many physicians viewed it as a cure-all for everything from stomach problems to asthma. Patients treated with the stimulant reported feeling less pain, more energy, and an overall sense of happiness and well-being.

In the late 1800s, drug companies were busily producing hundreds of thousands of pounds of cocaine. Not only was it easy to obtain, but countless doctors also claimed it was completely safe to use. In addition, famous figures ranging from Queen Victoria of England to American inventor Thomas Edison publicly praised the medical value of cocaine. Some physicians even insisted that it helped patients struggling with addiction to a painkiller called morphine. Within a few short years, however, people began to change their opinions.

Evidence of Abuse and Addiction

By the early 1900s, cocaine was starting to seem less like a wonder drug and more like the source of unexpected trouble.

10

UNEXPECTED ADDICTS

Many of the same notable people who initially praised cocaine and its euphoric effects later found themselves struggling with addiction. In several cases scientists conducted experiments with the drug by using it themselves. At first an Austrian doctor named Sigmund Freud—who eventually became famous for his theories about the human mind—could not speak highly enough of the stimulant. "A small dose lifted me to the heights in a wonderful fashion," he reported. Experts suspect that this realization was the starting point for Freud's twelve-year cocaine addiction, which he overcame in the late 1890s.

Well-respected American surgeon William Steward Halsted experienced similar problems with the drug at roughly the same time. It is not certain how his cocaine abuse began, but researchers suggest that it started while he was testing its effectiveness as an anesthetic during the final decades of the nineteenth century. Though Halsted made numerous scientific contributions that improved the practice of surgery, most experts doubt that he ever managed to conquer his drug addiction.

The number of Americans using the drug quintupled between 1890 and 1903—and not all of them were sick or undergoing surgery. People were drawn to the physical and mental sensations that cocaine produced, including euphoria and increased stamina.

In many cases it allowed laborers to work longer hours without feeling weak or exhausted. Some users also found cocaine cheaper and easier to obtain than alcohol. During the late 1800s, it was even a common ingredient in everyday items such as soft drinks, wine, ointments, and margarine.

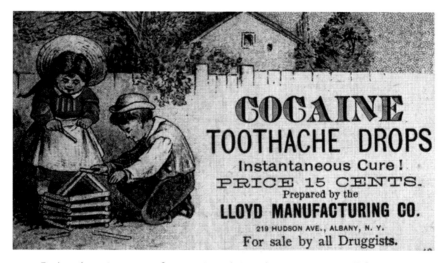

Early advertisements for cocaine claimed it was a cure-all for a number of ailments. In this advertisement from 1885, cocaine is presented as a cure for toothaches.

CONTROVERSIAL COCA-COLA

When a pharmacist named John Pemberton invented Coca-Cola in 1886, his intent was to create a non-alcoholic wine. The beverage was made using elements from various kola nuts, which provided caffeine, and coca leaves—which were a source of both flavorful syrup and cocaine. Pemberton added carbonated water, too, since many people believed it offered several health benefits.

At first the recipe for Coca-Cola featured a large amount of cocaine. Starting in the early twentieth century, however, manufacturers stopped adding it to the soft drink. Since they were eager to keep the flavor the coca leaves provided,

they simply extracted the cocaine and set it aside as a byproduct. This is essentially the same process that Coca-Cola currently relies upon, though it is strictly controlled by the US government. Nowadays the cocaine that is stripped from coca leaves is often distributed to medical companies for use in the production of anesthetics.

Americans gradually became aware that cocaine did far more than kill pain and boost energy. Throughout the early twentieth century, a growing number of medical journals contained reports of addiction to the drug. Doctors also began to notice that several patients who used cocaine seemed to suffer from nasal injuries and heart problems.

In addition, people started linking the stimulant with aggressive, unpredictable behavior and sometimes, violent criminal activity. Final proof that the drug was not the medical miracle that scientists had once imagined it to be came in 1912. Government officials estimated that roughly 5,000 deaths that year were related to cocaine abuse.

New Laws, New Narcotics

In 1914, American lawmakers passed an act intended to control the production and sale of cocaine and various other drugs. Fifty-six years later they declared that cocaine was both highly addictive and illegal, except when used as an anesthetic during certain surgeries. Despite these laws, cocaine regained popularity during the 1970s and 1980s. Dealers sold it illegally at $200 per gram, causing some people to believe that it was mainly a luxury of the rich and glamorous.

14

By the 1980s, however, crack became well known on America's streets. Crack is made by heating a mixture of powdered cocaine, water, and ammonia or baking soda. It is also sometimes referred to as "freebase." Since crack is cheap to produce—but still delivers an intense high— it frequently appeals to less wealthy users, including Americans living in poorer **urban** areas.

Any form of cocaine can quickly become addictive and dangerous. Trouble with the law is just one possible outcome of using this stimulant. Health issues ranging from nosebleeds to heart attacks are others. People who abuse cocaine also often suffer from mental disturbances and problems at work, school, and home. It is not uncommon for addicts to spend most or all of their income and savings to support their drug habit. For some users like Whitney Houston, the cost of abusing cocaine ultimately proves even greater.

CHAPTER TWO

A Stimulant's Deadly Strength

FORMER BOSTON CELTICS STAR CHRIS Herren remembers being "recruited [by] every school in [the] country" when he was just eighteen years old. Not long afterward he began playing basketball at Boston College in Chestnut Hill, Massachusetts—which was also where he first tried cocaine. Years later Herren admitted to being pressured to sample the stimulant by his roommate's girlfriend.

"She said . . . 'It's not going to kill you, I promise,'" he recalled. Herren swore it would be the last time he ever did cocaine, but the next fourteen years saw him repeatedly going back on his word. Along the way he got expelled from Boston College after testing positive for cocaine use. Herren was lucky enough to be given a second chance by a basketball coach at another school and was ultimately drafted by the Celtics. Yet his struggle with drug abuse continued for the next several years.

"I was a twenty-one-year-old cocaine addict," Herren reflected. Eventually he also started to use prescription drugs and heroin. Herren got high before important games. He based career decisions that involved relocating on how far away he'd be from

Chris Herren had a short-lived career as an NBA player. His addiction to drugs cost him his job and almost resulted in his death.

his drug dealer. The night his third child was born, he was too busy smoking crack to be at the hospital with his wife.

After destroying his career with the National Basketball Association (NBA) and overdosing on more than one occasion, Herren finally turned his life around. In the summer of 2008, he became sober. He now dedicates much of his time to speaking in public about his battle with drugs, including cocaine.

"I've been to hell and back," Herren recently noted. "I lived the life that most people . . . don't get a chance to come out of, straight up. By the grace of God and the help [of many] people, I was able to come out of this." While his story is inspiring, it also raises the question of what

In addition to writing *Basketball Junkie: A Memoir,* Chris Herren also travels the country speaking to young adults about his experience with drug addiction and recovery.

would drive a person to go to hell and back and sacrifice a promising future in the process. In Herren's case at least part of the answer is cocaine—a drug that overpowers the brain and often leads to the pain of addiction.

An Overview of Abuse

At first glance cocaine gives few clues that it is a deadly **narcotic**. This stimulant can take on a few different forms, depending on how it is processed. When combined with acids like hydrochloride, it often looks like a fine white powder. Crack, on the other hand, is sold in solid, shapeless chunks that range in color from off-white to brown. This version of cocaine usually resembles small crystals, pellets, or rocks.

Users typically inject, snort, or swallow powdered cocaine. Crack is almost always smoked. Powdered cocaine has various street names, including blow, nose candy, and powder. People commonly refer to crack as base, chalk, gravel, rock, or stones.

No matter what cocaine is called, which form it takes, or how it is abused, it presents countless risks to users. Whether the drug is

One of the reasons that crack is so dangerous is that it is extremely easy for users to overdose.

Cocaine and crack come in a variety of dangerous forms.

smoked, snorted, or injected, it ultimately enters a person's bloodstream. It is not unusual for people to feel its effects almost immediately, since cocaine generally reaches the brain within a matter of seconds.

Rewiring the Reward Circuit

Cocaine has a powerful impact on the parts of the human brain that regulate, or control, how someone experiences pleasure. These areas are often known as the brain's reward

20

There are few guarantees that cocaine is always the same product that dealers claim they are selling.

POISONOUS BLENDS AND IMPURITIES

They often cut, or mix, the powdered version of the drug with everything from cornstarch and sugar to flour and talcum powder. This allows dealers to sell more of the stimulant to users, who typically are not aware that they're paying for impurities. In other cases both crack and powdered cocaine are accidentally tainted with poisonous chemicals while they are being processed.

Sometimes users know that the drug they're purchasing lacks purity. These individuals actually seek out a mixture of substances that, when blended, frequently create more intense effects. For example, "speedball" is a potentially fatal mixture of cocaine and a highly addictive opioid called heroin. This killer combination was responsible for the deaths of actors John Belushi (1982), River Phoenix (1993), and Chris Farley (1997).

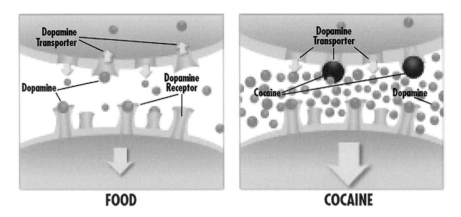

Cocaine generates a feeling of euphoria by building the amount of dopamine in the brain.

circuit. The drug interrupts normal activity within the reward circuit by attaching to nerve endings that affect how a brain chemical called **dopamine** is absorbed.

Dopamine works by carrying electrical impulses, or messages, between nerve cells that control movement, emotions, motivation, and pleasure. The brain usually produces dopamine in response to outside signals that it connects with feelings of satisfaction and enjoyment. Examples of these pleasurable triggers include the smell of a certain food that someone likes or the sound of his or her favorite type of music.

Normally nerve endings reabsorb extra dopamine. They almost perform a recycling process within the brain's

reward circuit. When cocaine attaches to nerve endings, however, this does not occur. As a result dopamine remains in the tiny gaps, or spaces, between nerve cells. This causes a person's dopamine levels to rise—which leads to increased energy and heightened feelings of pleasure. Cocaine has the same effect on other brain signals that control a person's sleep patterns, appetite, memory, mood, blood pressure, and heart rate.

Over time, however, the brain starts to respond to the abnormal activity in its reward circuit. It reacts to the high levels of dopamine by producing less of the chemical and shuts down the nerve endings that normally reabsorb it. This makes it harder for people to achieve the pleasurable effects they experienced when they first did cocaine. They often slip into addiction as they start using more drugs in an effort to create the same feelings of euphoria and alertness. Breaking this cycle is not easy. A person's brain becomes trained to repeat behaviors that activate its reward circuit—and this includes cocaine abuse.

It is not uncommon for cocaine addicts to go on binges when they use the stimulant over and over again for hours or days at a time. In general, the full effects of the drug last for anywhere from five to thirty minutes. Someone on a binge repeatedly abuses cocaine in an attempt to remain high for as long as possible.

IMMEDIATE EFFECTS

In most cases cocaine begins working immediately and causes users to be extremely alert to sensations such as sight, sound, and touch. Many people who abuse the drug say that, shortly after getting high, they feel less tired and hungry and tend to be more talkative and excitable. As their high starts to fade, however, they experience what is known as a "crash." During this period a person frequently suffers from hunger, exhaustion, depression, and anxiety.

Yet users face greater risks than crashing when they decide to abuse cocaine. The stimulant helps them feel energized and alert because it speeds up how their bodies operate. Cocaine raises blood pressure, heart rate, and body temperature. It forces a person's circulatory and nervous systems to work harder than normal, which often leads to an irregular heartbeat and disturbances to blood flow to the brain. This is why some people who abuse cocaine have heart attacks and strokes.

Unfortunately, many users of the drug do not consider that it is powerful enough to kill them. This is a dangerous

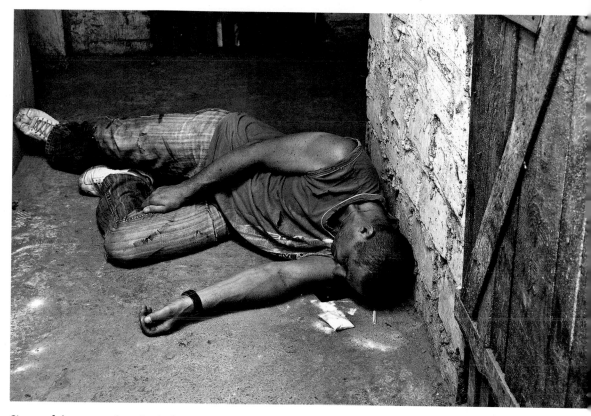

Signs of drug overdose include nausea, vomiting, seizures, and chest pain. Unless quickly treated, a drug overdose can lead to death.

assumption. A study conducted by the Centers for Disease Control and Prevention (CDC) indicated that 5,100 of the US deaths that occurred in 2008 were related to cocaine. Some of these fatalities were a result of overdose. Others were caused by the gradual—but still deadly—toll that cocaine takes on a person's physical and mental health.

DOUBLY DANGEROUS

Some users decide to try narcotics for the first time when they are at a party and under the influence of alcohol. Drinking and doing drugs always creates doubly dangerous health risks. Yet scientists have determined that this is especially true when it comes to mixing alcohol and cocaine. They have observed that a person's liver combines both substances to create a chemical called cocaethylene. While cocaethylene causes people to feel even more euphoric than if they did cocaine alone, it is also more likely to result in sudden death.

CHAPTER THREE

Horrifying and Harmful Impacts

COCAINE IS CAPABLE OF ROBBING USERS of every part of their identity—from appearance to personality. One recovering addict said that before she sought help, she barely recognized herself when looking in the mirror. She did not know who she was anymore, except that crack had set her on a path that would only end in disaster.

"I hadn't showered in two or three weeks," the former user acknowledged. "I was thin because I didn't eat a lot. I was dehydrated, [and] my face was drawn. . . . I felt like I knew I was dying." Similarly frightening stories describe the destructive physical and mental effects of cocaine abuse.

Some addicts have admitted to being so desperate to fund their habit that they've sold their children's toys or spent money on drugs, rather than food. Others have burned off their eyebrows or permanently scarred their fingertips while smoking crack. Cocaine abuse can lead to everything from **hallucinations** to heart failure. Whether in the form of powder or crack crystals, it has earned a well-deserved reputation for taking a heavy toll on users.

Hard on Physical Health

The impact that cocaine has on someone's physical health depends on several factors. These include how long a person has been taking the stimulant, how much of it they're using, and their method of abuse. For example, long-term addicts frequently suffer more health complications than individuals who have just tried cocaine for the first time. Yet it is important to understand that abusing this drug is always extremely dangerous!

Many of the negative effects on a user's body stem from the fact that using cocaine speeds up the brain and the nervous system. Constricted, or tightened, blood vessels and disruption to normal brain activity are common problems. So are increases in temperature, blood pressure, and

28

LONG-TERM TROUBLE

Health complications connected to cocaine abuse are not always obvious or immediate. Sometimes they develop over a long period of time and remain with a person even after he or she stops using. For instance, many cocaine addicts experience a hardening of their blood vessels. This can lead to blockages that impact how blood flows to important organs such as the heart, kidneys, lungs, and brain.

Another long-term health problem linked to cocaine abuse is poor nutrition. Since the stimulant decreases appetite, it is not uncommon for users to lose weight. Some also become dehydrated if they are not drinking and eating enough to support their already-overworked bodies.

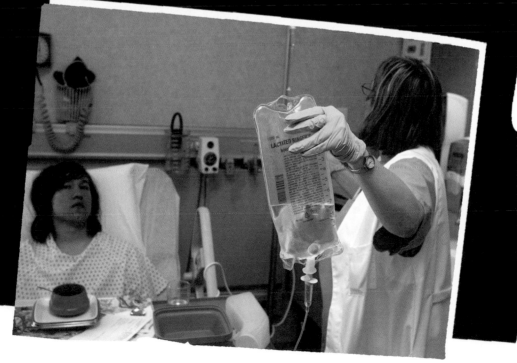

breathing and heart rate. Possible results of these bodily changes include seizures, heart attacks, strokes, and respiratory and kidney failure. In some cases, a first experience with cocaine can prove fatal. People often overdose because they are not aware of how even a small amount of the drug can put their body into overdrive.

Each particular method of cocaine abuse involves unique risks, as well. Swallowing the stimulant can destroy stomach tissue. People who snort cocaine frequently experience nosebleeds and difficulty breathing. Users sometimes report losing their sense of smell, too. Snorting can cause the complete collapse of their nasal septum, or the thin wall that divides a person's nose in half.

Smoking crack creates equally devastating health problems. This method of abusing cocaine irritates users' lungs and throat, and triggers a hacking cough. Crack addicts also report burning their fingers and face, and spitting up black **phlegm** and blood.

Injecting cocaine takes a similarly brutal toll on the body. Allergic reactions and skin infections are a few common side effects of this method of abuse. Yet sharing dirty needles can lead to even more serious consequences, including the spread of diseases such as **hepatitis** and

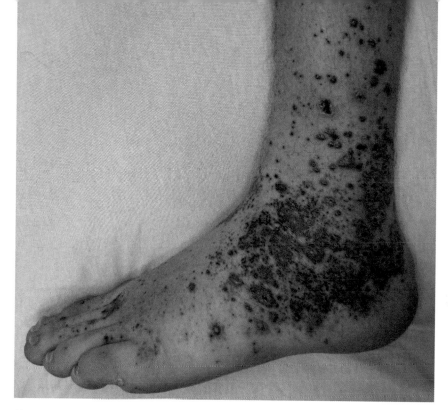

There are several negative side effects of cocaine abuse, including skin infections.

human immunodeficiency virus (HIV). Unfortunately, as a person's addiction to cocaine worsens, such health threats begin to matter less than the idea of getting high.

A Severely Altered Mental State

Cocaine impacts more than users' bodies. This stimulant also has terrifying effects on a person's mind and emotions. People who abuse cocaine often report feeling irritable, restless, and anxious—especially during the crash that follows a high.

The drug causes **paranoia** and hallucinations, too. Addicts frequently see and hear things that do not truly exist. They demonstrate fear, violence, and aggression in response to what they believe are threats. Yet many of the dangers that such individuals observe in the world around them are not real. Instead they are a result of the abnormal activity that is occurring within a user's brain.

Cocaine abuse also makes people act impulsively and irresponsibly. When high, they typically feel a heightened sense of confidence and super-human energy. A person under the influence of cocaine might therefore participate in risky behavior, such as unprotected sex, that he or she would probably avoid when sober.

The need to repeatedly get high also alters, or changes, users' behavior. Addicts come to value cocaine above all else, including the health and safety of their family and friends. Their habit eats away at whatever money they have, and they sometimes steal or commit other crimes to purchase drugs.

When cocaine addicts cannot figure out how to achieve their next high, their behavior can take a terrifying and unpredictable turn for the worse. Many become severely depressed. Others grow angry and aggressive as their need to use causes increased discomfort and anxiety. People

THE COST OF A COCAINE HABIT

In most areas a bag containing less than a gram of crack crystals sells for about $10 to $40. Powdered cocaine is more expensive and costs users approximately $80 to $100 per gram. Yet these prices are often only a starting point for serious addicts, who sometimes spend hundreds to thousands of dollars within a matter of days to pay for their habit.

suffering from hallucinations and paranoia are capable of lashing out at anyone or anything around them. Some even commit murder or suicide while in an altered mental state.

Working through Withdrawal

It is possible to overcome cocaine addiction, though this is not a simple or pleasant process. People often

Depression and anxiety are common symptoms of drug withdrawal.

incorrectly assume the opposite because **withdrawal** does not always involve obvious physical symptoms. Yet, according to many former addicts, reprogramming the brain to operate without cocaine is extremely challenging.

Withdrawal sometimes includes physical side effects such as shaking, muscle pain, and stomach problems. Certain addicts may feel exhausted, while others might be overly anxious and unable to sleep. Several users find that they become angry or depressed as their nervous system grows accustomed to an absence of cocaine.

The longer someone abuses this stimulant, the harder it may be for him or her to quit. Fortunately countless addicts have demonstrated that people possess enough inner strength to get clean and enjoy healthier, drug-free lives. Ultimately, however, most of them would probably agree that avoiding cocaine in the first place is the best way to escape the danger and devastation of addiction.

34

CHAPTER FOUR

Social Problems and Solutions

THERE ARE SEVERAL DIFFERENT REASONS why people make the decision to try cocaine. Some users abuse the stimulant in response to **peer pressure**. They find it difficult to say no when friends or classmates are getting high at a party because they're concerned about not fitting in. In other cases certain individuals do cocaine to escape reality. The drug causes them to feel more content and confident if they are suffering from depression or anxiety.

People also experiment with cocaine because they are drawn to its dark, glamorous image. They frequently hear news stories linking celebrities to the stimulant. In addition, many users are fascinated with the idea of the intense and unpredictable high that is commonly associated with cocaine. It appeals to their desire to both take risks and experience a rewarding rush.

Finally, a large number of people use cocaine because they do not know all the facts about it. Not everyone is aware that abusing the drug even once can result in serious consequences—including death. Some users understand this is possible but do not believe that they are vulnerable or that anything bad will ever happen to them. Yet, regardless of the exact reason that a person decides to try cocaine, hardly anyone ever plans on becoming an addict.

One college student at Yale University in New Haven, Connecticut, explained during an interview that she first snorted the stimulant at a party. Within a few years, she was getting high several times a week and described cocaine as "a great way to start the day." The fact that this drug is highly addictive is only part of what makes it so dangerous. Equally disturbing is the reality that cocaine is powerful enough to impact not just individual users but also their friends, families, and entire communities throughout America.

A Community and Family Crisis

"Crack cocaine breeds violence," James Craig—then the police chief of Portland, Maine—said as a warning to the city's residents in 2010. Craig, who had previously worked with the Los Angeles Police Department (LAPD) in California, understood how cocaine abuse could rock a community to its core. After a particularly busy week in the fall of 2010, he feared that he was already witnessing the drug's devastating impact in Portland. He noted that within a matter of days, two home invasions, three robberies, and a stabbing had taken place. Each incident involved suspects who were either fighting over crack or who were high on it.

"Crack cocaine will destroy this community if we don't stay ahead of it," Craig, who now serves as the chief of police in Detroit, Michigan, warned the people of Portland.

James Craig

"Once the gangs start territorializing where cocaine is sold, then we're going to see the real violence. I saw the devastation of drugs in [Los Angeles]. When crack cocaine came on the scene, the gangs and violence really erupted." What Craig witnessed, on both the east and west coasts, is not uncommon once cocaine abuse spreads within a community. The stimulant is connected to a culture of crime that has been known to overshadow major cities and small towns alike.

As Craig noted, rival gangs that sell cocaine frequently use violence to gain control of the drug trade in a certain area. Yet the gunfire of gang members is not the only reason that crime rises when cocaine gains popularity within a particular neighborhood. Addicts themselves are a big part of the issue. People desperate to score their next high will often steal or commit other crimes to pay for their cocaine habit. Since the stimulant can trigger hallucinations and paranoia, such individuals sometimes display aggressive, unpredictable behavior. All of these factors affect the safety and overall quality of life in communities where cocaine abuse occurs.

There are several other examples of how this narcotic impacts not just users but everyone around them as well.

The Country's Crack Epidemic

The word "epidemic" often describes the widespread outbreak of a disease. From the mid-1980s to the mid-1990s, however, people used the term to refer to crack's lightning-fast rise in popularity throughout major cities across America. A cheap way to achieve an intense high, the drug took urban areas by storm.

Before long, people reported a spike in crime and other social problems that they linked to crack addiction. Looking back, some experts believe that the media exaggerated the country's crack epidemic. Yet few can argue that, during the late twenty-first century, the narcotic had a devastating impact on US citizens, especially African Americans and the poor.

Studies show that doing cocaine increases the risk that someone will cause a car crash or an accident in the workplace. The drug is also linked to higher divorce rates, domestic abuse, and financial difficulty.

Cocaine strains personal relationships and has been known to rip entire families apart. As a person sinks deeper into his or her addiction, friends and loved ones frequently become less important than getting high. Users' changes in behavior leave emotional and sometimes physical scars on the people who care about them. It is not unusual for severe addicts to abuse, neglect, or even abandon their children as they lose sight of everything around them—except cocaine.

"I did not grow up with my mom," reported the teenage daughter of one such parent. "After she had me, she started using . . . cocaine. . . . [My parents] divorced when I was one. My older brothers and sisters . . . tell me about how nice she was before she got strung out. I finally got to meet my biological mom. . . . At fifty-three she is still using, has AIDS, and a habit of crying a lot. . . . What sucked the most is that she did not remember having me."

Efforts to Address a Problem

From the children of addicts to famous celebrities, Americans are working hard to fight the spread of cocaine abuse. A portion of their battle is trying to understand what drives people to do this drug in the first place. Another part of the struggle to stop cocaine use involves educating the public about how dangerous it actually is.

Police officers, teachers, parents, and kids have teamed up in several areas to learn and share the facts about this deadly stimulant. They hold meetings at town halls,

40

A rally held by the National Council on Alcoholism and Drug Dependence (NCADD).

community centers, and schools to discuss the best ways to keep the drug off their streets and out of their neighborhoods. One solution such groups have come up with is to make residents more aware of the warning signs of cocaine abuse.

Many school districts also sponsor drug-education programs that provide students with a better understanding of what the narcotic is and how it destroys young lives. In addition, doctors and other experts who deal with addiction encourage parents to talk to their children face-to-face about cocaine. Discussing the risks and consequences of using the stimulant and creating open, honest relationships lessens the odds that kids will ultimately abuse drugs.

Several non-profit organizations are attacking cocaine on a much larger scale. During the 1980s and 1990s, these groups arranged for action stars such as Clint Eastwood and Bruce Willis to make public service announcements (PSAs) warning television viewers not to try crack. More recently the non-profits have sponsored and created viral videos and Internet campaigns designed to have the same effect.

Finally, magazines, newspapers, and television programs sometimes feature famous athletes and performers discussing their past cocaine use. Celebrities ranging from Lady Gaga to Demi Lovato to Samuel L. Jackson often use these interviews to talk about how and why they conquered their drug problem. Their stories serve as shocking, powerful examples of how everyone is vulnerable to the effects of cocaine abuse and addiction.

Living with Legal Consequences

US lawmakers are also doing their part to address Americans' troubling relationship with cocaine. One of the countless risks that users do not think about when they first try the stimulant is that they are experimenting with an illegal narcotic. Fines and prison sentences connected to cocaine depend on a few different factors. These include how much of the drug a person is found with when he or she is arrested, as well as whether police believe any of it was intended for sale. Past criminal history shapes what punishment a judge decides, as well.

Drug users face the risk of jail or prison time.

STRICTER SENTENCING FOR CRACK?

Starting in the 1980s, federal judges handed down the same sentences for possessing either 1 gram of crack or 100 grams of powdered cocaine. Over time, though, it became clear that lawmakers needed to reconsider their position. Many legal experts argued that powdered cocaine was no less deadly than crack. In addition, several people felt the old sentencing policies were unfair to African Americans, who were found guilty of crack-related crimes more often than people of other races.

The U.S. government therefore decided to make some changes in 2010. Now prison time is similar for someone convicted of possessing either 1 gram of crack or 18 grams of powdered cocaine. Officials still do not consider these drugs identical, but they recognize that the second often proves just as lethal and habit-forming as the first.

Federal laws state that possession of more than 28 grams of crack—or 500 grams of powdered cocaine—will automatically earn someone at least five years behind bars. A person faces this sentence even if he or she has never been convicted of any previous offenses involving the stimulant. State laws dealing with possession of cocaine vary, but most result in $1,000 to $500,000 in fines and four to fifteen months in prison. Manufacturing or selling the narcotic typically leads to even stiffer punishments.

Crimes related to cocaine are regarded as serious offenses. People often do not realize that getting high poses a threat to more than their health. Abusing cocaine can rob them of their freedom, as well. It is one of many possible consequences that all serve as good reasons to reconsider using the drug.

CHAPTER FIVE

Conquering Cocaine Abuse

THE BEST METHOD OF AVOIDING THE worst side effects of cocaine abuse is to play it safe and stay away from the drug altogether. Unfortunately this is often easier said than done. It is sometimes difficult to refuse drugs when that decision means standing up to peer pressure. Luckily a few simple steps frequently make saying no easier.

For starters, people can steer clear of peer pressure by paying attention to who their peers are. It's important to have friends who understand the dangers of doing cocaine. Staying close to these individuals guarantees that that

Many teens are pressured into trying drugs by friends and acquaintances.

person is surrounded by a support network during social situations such as parties. On the other hand, it's never a bad idea to consider skipping get-togethers that involve drugs or alcohol and find a different way to have fun instead.

Of course, peer pressure is not the only reason that people abuse cocaine. Some users turn to the stimulant because they're attracted to the idea of a thrilling, unpredictable rush. Yet there are far better methods of experiencing this effect. Participating in a sports competition, performing in a play, or even inviting someone to a dance are all opportunities to feel similar—but safer—sensations.

Imagine a person starring in a school musical. The singer has been practicing her solo for weeks, but her heart is still pounding when the curtain rises. She knows she's taking a risk as she steps onstage. The director and the rest of the cast are counting on her to amaze the audience with her vocal skills. If her voice cracks or she forgets the lyrics of the song, she might let them down. Her cheeks flush as she begins singing, yet she ultimately delivers an impressive, powerful performance. There is a moment of silence when she finishes—followed by thundering applause! The singer feels an exhilarating rush of pride and relief once she realizes that her solo has been a success.

It is possible to enjoy activities that do not involve life-threatening behavior but feature risks and rewards all the same. People often experience both increased energy levels and intense euphoria when they set and fulfill a goal or overcome a difficult

Participating in healthy and fulfilling activities such as music and sports is one way to avoid the pitfalls of drugs.

challenge. In addition, this kind of "high" is better for the body and longer lasting than the effects of cocaine.

Yet not everyone starts abusing the stimulant because they are thrill-seekers intrigued by a dark, dangerous drug. Some people use cocaine as a kind of crutch that they believe will help them deal with life's troubles. Getting high causes certain individuals to feel more confident and

Some people turn to drugs in order to avoid their problems, but abuse and addiction only makes things worse.

self-assured—as if they could conquer the world. Eventually, cocaine actually makes most problems even more complicated. Its effects do not last forever, and users inevitably have to cope with both addiction and whatever difficult situation drove them to drugs in the first place.

Instead of escaping reality by doing cocaine, a person can deal with life's challenges by talking to a friend, family member, or teacher. Counselors, coaches, and doctors are a few other options. Many people also find that exercise, **meditation**, and journaling are good ways to sort out their emotions, as well as to gain increased energy and focus. No matter how someone decides to address their problems, it is important to remember that cocaine never offers safe or effective solutions in the long run.

Addressing Addiction

People who use cocaine often only realize the power of the drug once they are struggling with addiction. Luckily some of these individuals have the opportunity to turn their lives around before it is too late. Even severe addicts are capable of overcoming cocaine abuse, but it's important to get help as soon as possible. A successful recovery depends on supportive family and friends, too.

Kids are less likely to use drugs if they talk about them in an honest and open manner with family and friends.

If someone has been doing cocaine for a long time, it's wise to see a doctor. A physician can address any health issues that may have arisen as a result of risky behavior such as sharing needles. Doctors may also be able to advise users about the treatment plan that best fits their needs. Trained school counselors, and hotlines and websites that deal with drug abuse are excellent resources, as well.

It is not uncommon for cocaine addicts to initially deny that they have a problem. In these cases their loved ones sometimes have to arrange an intervention to convince them that they are in trouble and must seek help. Most interventions involve a user's family and friends working with a drug counselor or healthcare professional. They come together as a group to confront a person about their cocaine habit.

The goal of an intervention is not to embarrass someone who is suffering from addiction. People stage interventions to encourage users to participate in **rehabilitation**, or rehab. They want to persuade a person they care about to face up to their drug abuse and take whatever steps are necessary to start enjoying a cocaine-free life.

There are different forms of rehab that are each designed to fit an addict's individual situation and needs. Inpatient programs usually mean that former users live at a hospital, counseling center, or treatment facility. This type of treatment plan tends to be most effective for people who are battling long-term addiction or experiencing urgent health risks. Inpatient care allows counselors and medical staff to pay close attention to a person's physical and mental recovery. It is frequently the safest option if someone has recently survived an overdose. The majority of inpatient programs last about thirty days, but some are longer or shorter.

People are generally in outpatient treatment for a greater time period, which runs anywhere from two to

twelve months. They continue to live at home but regularly visit a hospital or counseling center to address their cocaine addiction. An outpatient plan may work best for users whose drug abuse does not pose an immediate threat to their safety or the safety of others. It is not uncommon for someone to start off in an inpatient program and later move on to outpatient care.

Both kinds of treatment plans frequently involve former addicts participating in **therapy**. A person who does therapy explores why he or she began abusing cocaine and reflects upon how to avoid using in the future. Therapy sessions may either be private or take place in a group setting with other people battling addiction. Family and friends sometimes join in therapy, as well. They talk to their loved ones about how cocaine has impacted their relationship and discuss different ways to rebuild trust and honesty.

Tackling cocaine abuse requires courage and determination, no matter what approach a person relies upon to recover. Several former addicts report struggling with the urge to use even after they complete treatment. Yet many of these individuals ultimately succeed in proving that they are more powerful than cocaine.

Education and Awareness

When Whitney Houston died in early 2012, much of the world responded with shock and sadness. At the same time, however, her death served as more than a surprising tragedy. It reminded people that cocaine can take over anyone's identity and that getting high is not worth the price that users often pay. Apart from Houston's unforgettable songs and performances, her legacy also includes increased awareness about the danger of drugs.

Knowing the facts about cocaine can make a life-or-death difference when someone has to decide whether or not to use. That is why it is so important to share information about this stimulant with others. There are several ways to spread the word about how cocaine kills.

Kids can team up with school and community leaders to educate the public. One possible method of raising awareness is to design posters and fliers explaining what crack and powdered cocaine are and the effects they produce. These special bulletins should list warning signs that suggest a person is using, as well as phone numbers for local treatment centers. They should ideally be hung in any public places where they are likely to capture the attention of others.

Teens play an important role in helping raise awareness about drugs and offering support to young people who are already struggling with addiction.

Another approach to increasing awareness about cocaine is to arrange a neighborhood or town meeting. Guest speakers might include police officers, doctors, drug counselors, and possibly even former addicts. All of these individuals can usually share information and tips that help prevent or stop the spread of cocaine abuse within a community.

The biggest mistake that people often make is to assume that cocaine will never impact them. Far too many users have underestimated the powder and crystals that are clearly capable of causing pain, destruction, and death. Yet by understanding what cocaine is—and that it is not worth dying for—a person becomes more powerful than this dangerous and deadly drug.

WATCH FOR WARNING SIGNS!

What are the warning signs that someone might be using cocaine? This chart lists several clues that often hint at cocaine abuse:

APPEARANCE

- Takes less interest in physical appearance-may bathe less often and change clothes less frequently
- Is pale or has dark shadows under the eyes
- Has glassy eyes with extremely large pupils
- Has unexplained scars, cuts, sores, burns, or bruises on face, hands, arms, and legs
- Has cracked, dry lips
- Has a red, irritated nose

HEALTH

- Suddenly coughs, sneezes, or sniffles more than usual
- Loses weight without exercising or dieting (cocaine abuse can affect one's appetite)
- Has unexplained stomach problems
- Sweats frequently and suffers from dehydration
- Has infected skin or flesh wounds
- Gradually experiences a growing number of dental issues (a frequent result of smoking crack)
- Seems to get sick more often than normal (sharing dirty needles can lead to the spread of several different illnesses and diseases)

SUSPICIOUS ITEMS

- Steel wool pads, baking soda, glass pipes, and matches (used for smoking crack)
- Glass mirrors, razors, straws, and rolled-up paper or dollar bills with traces of white powder on them (used for snorting cocaine)
- Needles that someone does not need to own for a specific medical reason (used to "shoot-up," or inject cocaine)
- Any unusual powder, rocks, or crystals (which may be concealed in baggies, paper, or foil)

BEHAVIOR

- Talks a lot and at a rapid pace; frequently switches topics during a conversation
- Appears hyperactive, anxious, or unable to relax
- Becomes irritable more easily than usual
- Displays unpredictable episodes of aggression or violence
- Seems paranoid or talks about seeing or hearing people, objects, or situations that don't truly exist
- Spends less time with family and friends and more time in the company of people who are known to use drugs
- Complains of financial troubles or frequently asks to borrow money
- Is caught stealing or abusing drugs
- Sets elaborate plans or goals but suddenly loses interest in following through on any of them
- Shows less interest in former activities and responsibilities at school, work, and home
- Is late or absent to routine events more often than normal

Glossary

addicted physically or mentally dependent on a particular substance

anesthetic a drug that causes temporary loss of bodily sensations

cocaine a powerful stimulant made from powder extracted from the leaves of the coca plant

crack a variant of cocaine that is smoked in the form of small rocks or crystals

dealers people who sell illegal drugs

dependent having an intense emotional or physical need for something

dopamine a brain chemical that carries electrical signals between nerve cells that control movement, emotions, motivation, and pleasure

euphoria a feeling of intense excitement and happiness

hallucinations visions of things that do not really exist

hepatitis a disease that causes sufferers to have a painful, swollen liver

human immunodeficiency virus (HIV) an incurable virus that attacks the body's white blood cells, making it hard to fight off infections; HIV causes a serious disease called acquired immunodeficiency syndrome (AIDS)

illegal against the law

meditation a mental exercise involving deep thinking and peaceful reflection that increase a person's overall focus and relaxation

narcotic a drug that tends to cause sleep, reduce pain, affect mood and behavior, and proves addictive when used for nonmedical purposes

overdose taking such an excessively dangerous amount of a certain drug that the body begins to shut down, sometimes resulting in death

paranoia a mental state in which a person perceives threats or dangers that do not really exist

peer pressure words or actions from people of the same age group that suggest a person has to act or look like them to fit in

phlegm a thick, sticky fluid that is produced within a person's respiratory system

rehabilitation treatment for drug or alcohol abuse

sober not affected by alcohol or drugs

stimulant a drug that temporarily speeds up how a person's bodily systems operate

therapy counseling designed to help a person overcome a negative behavior such as drug abuse

urban located within a city

withdrawal symptoms that occur when a person who is physically dependent on a drug stops using it

Find Out More

BOOKS

Bickerstaff, Linda. *Cocaine: Coke and the War on Drugs*. New York: Rosen Publishing Group, 2009.

Espejo, Roman, ed. *Chemical Dependency*. Detroit: Greenhaven Press, 2011.

Friedman, Lauri S., ed. *Drug Abuse*. Detroit: Greenhaven Press, 2012.

Hollander, Barbara. *Addiction*. New York: Rosen Publishing Group, 2012.

Marshall Cavendish Reference. *Drugs of Abuse*. New York: Marshall Cavendish, 2012.

———. *Substance Abuse, Addiction, and Treatment*. New York: Marshall Cavendish, 2012.

West, Krista. *Cocaine and Crack*. New York: Chelsea House Publishers, 2008.

Websites

Center for Substance Abuse Treatment (CSAT)

www.samhsa.gov/about/csat.aspx

> CSAT is a good resource for finding a local treatment center that deals with cocaine abuse and addiction.

KidsHealth—What You Need to Know about Drugs: Cocaine and Crack

kidshealth.org/kid/grow/drugs_alcohol/know_drugs_cocaine.html

> Review this site for additional fast facts on powdered cocaine and crack.

The National Institute on Drug Abuse (NIDA) for Teens—Mind over Matter: Cocaine

teens.drugabuse.gov/mom/mom_stim1.php

> This NIDA site provides a closer look at how cocaine impacts the human brain.

Index

Pages in **boldface** are illustrations

About the Author

KATIE MARSICO has written more than 100 books for children and young adults. Before becoming a full-time author she worked as a managing editor. Marsico lives in a suburb of Chicago, Illinois, with her husband and five children.